FEET
(not to scale)

(Right foot is shown in each case). Adapted to the sort of life the bird lives and to its habitat.

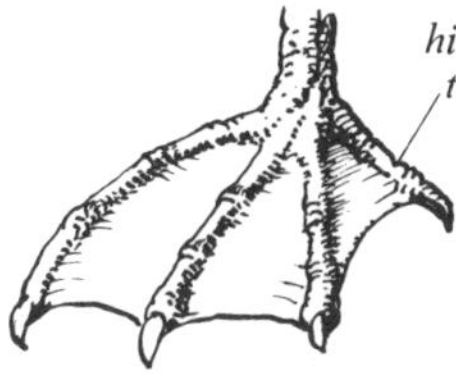

CORMORANT
All four toes are webbed. This is a bird which swims on and under water.

... ground.

... ort. ... but ... ich ... ing. Bird spends most time on the wing.

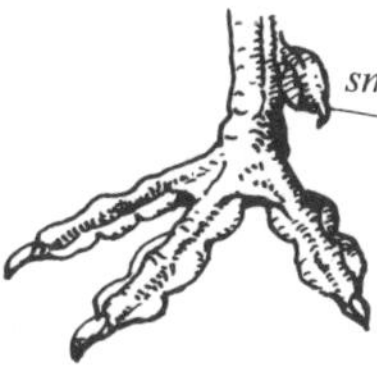

PHALAROPE
Lobed toes and partial web. Bird swims, wades and runs.

PLOVER
Toes are not webbed and hind toe is often absent. Bird walks and runs.

SAND MARTIN
All four toes face forwards. Bird uses them for grasping rock face, etc.

EGGS
(not to scale)

The shape adapted to the type and site of nest.

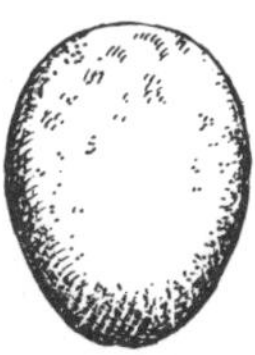

PUFFIN
Lays egg in burrows. Normal egg shape.

GUILLEMOT lays egg on a cliff ledge. Shape of egg prevents it from rolling away– it will roll in a circle.

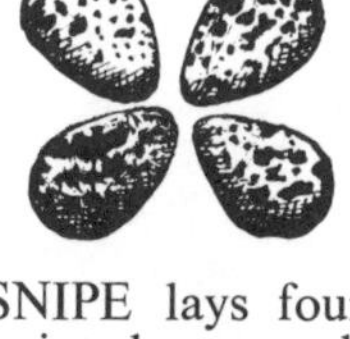

SNIPE lays four pointed eggs and, like other birds which do the same, arranges them as shown in order to cover them in the smallest possible space.

Series 536

John Leigh-Pemberton's superb illustrations will help children — and adults — to identify more positively the birds they see around our coasts and estuaries. The clear, interesting and reliable text will doubtless stimulate many people to take an even greater interest in bird life.

SEA and ESTUARY BIRDS

by

JOHN LEIGH-PEMBERTON

Ladybird Books Loughborough

Storm Petrel

Petrels, Shearwaters and Fulmars are birds of the ocean, which come to land only when driven in by storms, or for nesting. All have nostrils of a special kind, arranged as tubes at the base of the bill.

The Storm Petrel is our smallest sea bird and the smallest bird with webbed feet, which it sometimes trails along the surface of the water as it flies. It can be seen doing this, with a rather bat-like motion, as it follows in the wake of a ship. This little bird, not much bigger than a House Martin, is known as 'Mother Carey's Chicken' and was once supposed to foretell the coming of bad weather at sea.

Nesting activity, on various islands from the Scilly Isles to northern Scotland, takes place chiefly at night and in small colonies. A single egg is placed in a burrow, or a crevice among rocks, and the chick is fed, to begin with, on a musky smelling oil which both parents produce. This oil can also be ejected as a means of defence when the bird is alarmed, and the nesting place can be detected by its peculiar smell. There is only one brood, and the chick is unable to fly until it is two months old.

Manx Shearwater *(above)*

Fulmar *(below)*

The commonest of the four Shearwaters found off our coasts is the Manx Shearwater which, in spite of its name, is no longer found in the Isle of Man. It breeds, usually in a burrow, on islands off our western coast, but occurs on other coasts all round Britain. Only one egg is laid, and the parents take it in turns to incubate in spells of from seven to ten days, during which time they do not feed. The young bird, hatched in about eight weeks, is deserted after sixty days and remains in the burrow, untended, until it can fly some two weeks later.

Shearwaters fly close to the water in a series of glides, often cutting the surface with a wing-tip . . . hence their name.

Fulmars are also superb fliers, flapping more than Shearwaters (to which they are related) and looking much more like gulls. Like Petrels, they can eject a musky smelling oil when angry, but their nesting habits are different. The Fulmar nests in colonies: principally on St. Kilda, but in recent years on other cliffs of the Scottish coasts. A single egg is laid in a rough nest on a ledge or cliff top.

Fulmars, Shearwaters and Petrels make a curious assortment of cries, nearly always at the nest.

Cormorant

Although the Cormorant is chiefly a bird of the coast, it can quite often be found on river banks or on the shore of a loch. It is with us throughout the year and frequents almost every coast.

This large bird—it is about three feet long—is a superb fisherman and diver, capable of staying submerged for as long as a minute and using its strong feet, which are webbed between all four toes, to swim under water. Its diet consists almost entirely of fish, of which it eats some six pounds daily. In the Far East the Cormorant has for centuries been used by man to dive for fish, a collar being fitted to prevent the bird from swallowing its catch.

Cormorants are most often seen flying low over the water, or perched on a rock or post with wings 'hung out to dry'. They are usually silent but are capable of a harsh sound—'kaark'. They nest in colonies on rocks or cliffs (but not in the south-east of England); three or four eggs are laid in a nest made chiefly of seaweed, and incubation takes about four weeks. There is only one brood, and the young remain in the nest for more than a month.

Shag *(above)*

Gannet *(below)*

The Shag is a smaller version of the Cormorant, and in its habits is similar in most ways. But it is not found inland or near rivers, spending all its time near the sea, where it is even more at home than the Cormorant, particularly in rough weather. Unlike the Cormorant, it has a curved crest on its head and no white in its plumage. Normally three eggs are laid in a nest which, made chiefly of rotting seaweed, is remarkable both for its dreadful smell and also for the Shag's habit of decorating the nest with flowers or leaves.

Gannets are fine, big birds, found in crowded colonies on ledges of precipitous cliffs. The chief colonies, which are often huge, are in Scotland, but there are others in Wales and Ireland. The Gannet is strictly a maritime bird, resident throughout the year, and is notable for its spectacular method of fishing. From any height up to a hundred feet it will dive headlong, wings half open but finally fully closed as it hits the water with enormous force. The fish, even at a depth of several feet, is impaled and eaten under water.

Gannets lay one egg in a nest of seaweed and turf. When not nesting they spend their whole lives at sea.

Razorbill *(above)*

Guillemot *(below)*

These two birds belong to the Auk family, which also includes the Little Auk, the Puffin and two other kinds of Guillemot. All are marine birds which come ashore only to breed. Most of them have particularly small wings, which cause them to fly with rapid wing beats, but which are used to great effect as aids to swimming under water. This family has very varied and curious beaks, and they walk upright—but somewhat awkwardly.

The Razorbill is a resident bird of the coast, coming to land to breed from spring until August. The single egg is laid in May in a rock crevice, and large colonies, often in company with Guillemots, are formed. These are to be found on most rocky or cliff-bound coasts of the north and west. Neither Razorbills nor Guillemots breed on our eastern or south-eastern shores.

Guillemots, which are also resident birds, prefer to breed on cliff ledges or on flat-topped rock formations. There is one egg which can be very variable in colour, blue-green, reddish or white; and the chick is tended by both parents, often with the help of the other birds in the colony.

Both these birds utter a cawing cry, which in a colony can cause a great deal of noise.

Puffin *(below)*

Kittiwake *(above)*

The Puffin is a member of the Auk family, and is notable for its massive, highly coloured bill. It comes to land only to breed, which it does in huge numbers in colonies at many sites from the Isle of Wight, round the south-west and western coasts, and up as far as Shetland. The nest is in a burrow, sometimes that of a rabbit, and one egg is laid. The chick is tended by both parents, but before it can fly or swim is deserted and has to find its own way to the sea. Outside the breeding period the Puffin spends its life at sea, often hundreds of miles from land.

Another bird seen far out in the ocean is the Kittiwake, which has been known to follow ships right across the Atlantic. It gets its name from its cry—' kitta-wa-ak ' which can be heard at nesting sites. These are in colonies, usually on steep cliffs, and the nests, made of seaweed, moss and grass, are neater than those of most sea birds. One to three eggs are laid and, as with other gulls, there is only one brood.

Unlike most other gulls, the Kittiwake is an expert fisherman, although it will also eat worms or grass. Because it lives many miles from land for so long it can drink sea-water when fresh water is not available.

Herring Gull *(juvenile above, adult below)*

The Herring Gull is probably the commonest member of its family in Britain; it is a resident, and is found on all coasts and sometimes inland as well. Like most other gulls, the plumage of the young differs from that of adults and changes every year until after the third year, when adult plumage is assumed. Many species of gulls are very alike when in juvenile plumage, and this makes it difficult to tell them apart. Gulls eat a certain amount of marine food, such as shell-fish, which is broken open by being dropped on to rocks; other food includes insects, worms, carrion, small mammals and even other sea-birds or their eggs. Many live largely on offal.

Breeding takes place during May, and the large nest is made of grass and seaweed. This is usually in a colony on cliffs, but sometimes Herring Gulls will nest on roofs. As with many other gulls the average number of eggs is three. Incubation, which takes twenty-seven days, is by both parents who share the feeding until the young can fly at about six weeks old.

The cries of all gulls are loud and very varied, a long wailing sound or a harsh yelp being typical. They are masterly fliers, capable of gliding, soaring and hovering as well as powerful, direct flight.

Common Gull *(above)*

Black-headed Gull *(below)*

It is often difficult to tell apart the various species of gulls. The best guide is to look for size, colour of bill and legs, and the markings of wing-tips, back and head.

The Common Gull is a resident whose numbers are increased in winter by visiting birds. It is 'common' only in the north and in Scotland and Ireland, although there is one breeding colony at Dungeness. The Common Gull is smaller than the Herring Gull and less heavily built, but in behaviour is generally similar to other gulls. Nesting, however, takes place on the ground, often some distance from the sea, and it is found at all times near large stretches of inland water. Its cry is a high-pitched, laughing 'kee-ak'.

The Black-headed Gull is really brown headed, and this only in the summer; in the winter the head is white with a dark mark behind the eye. This is a much smaller, daintier bird than the Common Gull. It is found almost everywhere and breeds not only on all coasts but to a large extent as much as twenty miles inland. It will nest in a swamp or on dry ground, on a roof or even in a tree. Like other gulls it raises only one brood, usually from three eggs. It will eat almost anything, particularly insects, as when following the plough.

Glaucous Gull *(above)*

Great Black-backed Gull *(below)*

These are the two largest British gulls, both fierce, ravenous birds which prey upon other sea-birds, their eggs and young.

The Glaucous Gull, a winter visitor, comes chiefly to our northern and north-eastern coasts. It breeds right round the Arctic Circle, and is commonly seen near whaling stations. The juveniles of this species differ from other gulls by being at all stages much paler, a creamy colour instead of mottled brown, and by the fact that they do not assume adult plumage until the fifth year. In other respects the Glaucous is much like the Great Black-backed Gull.

The Great Black-backed Gull is a resident, breeding on our south-western, western and northern coasts. It is not very common, but is easily recognised by its sturdy build and great size. It is often nearly thirty inches long, with a deep, hoarse cry—'och-och-och'. As well as killing other sea-birds, it also preys upon rabbits, rats and even lambs. It will take insects and worms, and is a skilled fisherman. The nest is large, built of seaweed, heather and grass, and usually placed among rocks or on cliff ledges, either singly or in a colony, often among other sea-birds. It is a graceful and powerful flier with wonderful control, even in the strongest wind.

Lesser Black-backed Gull *(above)*

Arctic Skua *(below)*

The Lesser Black-backed Gull is really a smaller, paler version of the Great Black-backed Gull. There are two forms of this bird occurring in Britain; one, a summer visitor, breeds here, and the other, which is slightly darker, is a Scandinavian bird which visits us in winter. The British form is fairly common and, recently, increasing numbers have become resident. It is found on most coasts and very frequently inland, where it follows the plough, and also gathers in some numbers on refuse dumps. Its nesting habits are similar to those of other gulls.

The Arctic Skua is a bird of the Polar regions occurring here at the edge of its natural range. It is therefore not common but breeds in the north of Scotland and the Scottish Islands. The nest, a hollow among heather or turf, contains two olive green eggs and these are valiantly defended by the parent birds, who will dive repeatedly at any intruder. There is only one brood.

Skuas are hawk-like birds and their flight is strong and very fast. This speed is used to chase other birds, such as gulls and terns, until they drop the food they are carrying; the Skua then swoops on the food, catching it in mid-air.

Arctic Tern *(top)*

Common Tern *(top centre)*

Sandwich Tern *(lower centre)*

Little Tern *(below)*

Terns are small, slender-winged birds with thin bills and forked tails. They are marvellous fliers and can hover above the water when feeding until they see a fish; they then dive, picking the fish neatly from the water. All have black caps in summer but not in winter. The different species are best told apart by the colouring of their feet and bills, and by the varying length of the outer feathers of their tails. All the Terns shown here are summer visitors to various parts of our coasts and all breed here. They nest in colonies on shingle, sand or grass, and two or three eggs are usual; there is only one brood.

The Arctic Tern probably travels farther than any bird in the world, ranging from the Arctic, where it breeds, to the Antarctic, where it winters at sea.

The Common Tern is the one most widely distributed in Britain, and can be found inland as well as on the coast. It is whiter underneath than the Arctic Tern, which tends to be greyish.

The Sandwich Tern (first recorded at Sandwich, Kent in 1784) is the largest of our breeding Terns, very white looking, with a less forked tail and long, tuft-like feathers behind the head. It winters in the Indian Ocean.

The Little Tern is the smallest, always with a white forehead.

Red-necked Phalarope (*above*)
winter and summer plumage

Grey Phalarope (*below*)
winter and summer plumage

Phalaropes are small waders, in many ways very different from other members of that family. They swim more than other waders, and feed while swimming not only out at sea but, during the breeding season, on inland waters as well. They spin round on the surface in order to stir up food from below; they 'up-end' like a duck or will seize insects in the air like a gull. Strong fliers, they are capable of flying from the Arctic Circle to the South Atlantic where they spend the winter far out at sea. They are curiously tame and can be watched quite closely.

A few Red-necked Phalaropes breed in northern Scotland, otherwise they are fairly scarce visitors, usually in the summer, but a few come in autumn, when they are in winter plumage. They nest in colonies on marshy ground, and about four eggs are laid. The male, which is smaller and duller than the female, incubates the eggs and tends the young, the female taking no part.

The Grey Phalarope does not breed in Britain, but comes here as a rare autumn visitor while on migration: Occasionally a few stay on into the winter, usually on our south and east coasts. It is thus normally seen here in grey winter plumage.

Golden Plover *(above)*

Ringed Plover *(below)*

Plovers are round-headed birds with thin bills and striking plumage. All of them like open spaces, and most of them spend some time on shores or estuaries. Their flight is rapid and they perform complicated aerial manoeuvres, but they also run about on the ground, particularly when feeding.

The Golden Plover is a resident bird which breeds chiefly on the moorlands of northern England and Scotland. In autumn and winter it comes in flocks to the coasts and estuaries. It feeds on insects and seeds as well as on small kinds of marine creatures. The Golden Plover's cry, uttered in flight, is a very pretty, whistling 'thui', and there is also an attractive, rippling song.

Much smaller is the Ringed Plover which is more typically a shore bird, found throughout the year on most coasts, where it mixes with other waders. It breeds among shingle or sand, the nest being no more than a depression, although it will sometimes line or surround this with small stones or shells. As with other plovers, three or four marvellously camouflaged eggs are laid, incubated by both parents. But the Ringed Plover produces two or even three broods, while other plovers are normally single-brooded. The cries and song of this most attractive little bird are low and melodious.

Turnstone *(above)*

Oystercatcher *(below)*

The Turnstone is a little bird which does not breed here, but some can be found throughout the year on all our coasts. It breeds from Greenland to Siberia and migrates to South Africa and Australia, an enormous journey for a bird no more than nine inches long. Its name comes from its feeding habit, for it runs about, turning over stones and seaweed and picking up whatever marine life is underneath. Its bill, which is slightly up-turned, is specially adapted for this method. It has a twittering cry or a precise ' keeoo-keeoo ' but is on the whole a silent bird, busy, pugnacious and capable of surprisingly rapid flight.

The Oystercatcher is a resident bird, commoner in the north than in the south of Britain. It is almost entirely a sea-shore bird, probing with its long bill for its food of shell-fish, shrimps and worms. By day and night, Oystercatchers are active and noisy, with a variety of shrill cries—' keep-keep '.

Oystercatchers nest on the shore as a rule, but sometimes will nest inland among heather. The nest is never more than a hollow, thinly lined with small stones or vegetation. Three eggs are normal, and the family is raised by both parents. There is only one brood, and the young birds can fly in about five weeks.

Sanderling *(top)*

Little Stint *(centre)*

Knot *(below)*

The Sanderling becomes extremely white in winter, when some birds remain here. It also occurs in small numbers in summer, but not often in the north of Britain. This busy little bird feeds very close to the water's edge; on migration it rivals the Little Stint in the length of its journey—a return trip almost from Pole to Pole each year.

The Little Stint, less than six inches long, is our smallest wader, commonest in the east and south of England. It occurs in varying numbers in autumn and in spring, and its winter plumage is grey above and white below, as with many other waders. Its flight is very rapid and, like other members of this family, flocks perform spectacular aerial evolutions in formation.

The Knot is a common bird of our east and north-western coasts, often in flocks of thousands. It favours large mud-flats or stretches of sandy beach, and some birds winter here; a few non-breeding birds remain in the summer, when the summer plumage can be seen. The winter plumage is grey and white. This is quite a tame bird, which gets its name from its cry—'knut-knut'.

These three waders are members of the Sandpiper family, autumn visitors here on migration from northern Europe to the Southern Hemisphere. None of them breeds here.

Black-tailed Godwit (*above*)
Common Sandpiper (*below*)

These are two more members of the Sandpiper family, which can be found in various forms all over the world.

The Black-tailed Godwit, a most beautiful and graceful bird, used to be only a rare visitor to Britain but has lately become more regular and more numerous. Now many birds spend the winter here, especially in the south, and some have begun to breed in various places. This is a bird which likes estuaries and mud-flats rather than the shore, and its nests are apt to be among vegetation. These nests are quite large structures made of grass and sometimes lined with leaves and feathers. Four eggs are laid, and one brood raised annually. The cry is ' wicka-wicka-wicka ', uttered loudly in flight.

The Common Sandpiper is a summer visitor, breeding here chiefly in Scotland and the northern and western English counties. It winters in Africa and even Australia. The winter plumage is less grey than with some other waders. The nest is a hollow lined with grass, anywhere from the shore to a cornfield, and often slightly raised. There are four eggs and one brood.

A distinguishing feature of the Common Sandpiper is its flight; this is low over the water and consists of a series of fluttering wing-beats followed by a short glide.

Snipe *(above)*

Curlew *(below)*

The Snipe is a resident bird throughout Britain, and in winter the population is increased by the arrival of migrating birds. Any wet area is a suitable habitat, preferably marshes but including the sea-shore. The Snipe is not often seen, as it is a bird which feeds at dusk and hides, absolutely still if necessary, during the day. When disturbed it rises with a loud cry—' skaap '—and, until out of danger flies in a rapid zig-zag.

The courtship display includes the curious ' drumming ', the bird diving at about forty-five degrees and a vibrating noise being made by the air striking the two protruding outer tail feathers. The nest is on the ground, and four eggs are hatched by the female; sometimes there are two broods. Snipe are rather solitary birds but occasionally form a flock—known as a ' wisp '.

The Curlew, another member of the Sandpiper family, is a large wader which lives usually on mud-flats and estuaries. It is a resident, breeding in favourable localities often in a position from which a look-out can be kept. There is one brood of about four eggs. The nest, slightly lined with grass, is a hollow on the ground.

The Curlew's cry is very distinctive, a sad, whistling ' cour-lee, cour-lee '. There is also a lovely, bubbling song. The slow, ponderous wing-beats produce a surprisingly rapid flight.

Redshank (*above*)

Dunlin (*below*)

The Redshank is a common, resident member of the Sandpiper family; rather a shy bird, it is most easily recognised in flight, when the large areas of white on tail and wing can be seen. It is notable too for its whistling cry—'tuu'—and the more elaborate yodel, uttered in flight which accompanies a dancing courtship display. Redshanks inhabit marshes and estuaries, but are also found in winter on the sea-shore. The nest is rather unusual for a wader, being built of grass with a sort of grass canopy over the top. There is a single brood of four eggs which take about three weeks to hatch. The hen, in particular, often refuses to leave her eggs, even to the extent of allowing herself to be picked up.

The Dunlin, of the same family, is a little wader which mixes freely with other birds of the marsh or shore, and can be found in many differing localities. It is a resident, breeding chiefly in Scotland on both marshes and moors. The nest is concealed, and four eggs of very variable colour are laid. There is one brood.

The Dunlin has a weak cry—'treep', but flocks utter a typical trilling sound. These flocks, flying in unison like wisps of smoke, perform marvellously controlled manoeuvres.

Rock Pipit ***(above)***

Shore Lark ***(hen and cock, below)***

The Rock Pipit is a resident bird, common on all rocky coasts; it belongs to the same family as the Wagtails. It is an active bird, which runs about exploring seaweed for flies and small shrimps. It has a fluttering flight and is apt to ' float ' on the air as if being blown along downwind—a rather useful distinguishing feature of an otherwise rather drab little bird. Normally two broods are raised. The four or five eggs are laid in a nest nearly always fairly close to the shore and hidden in a rock crevice. The song—' wheet-wheet-tre-zee-zee '—is uttered in flight, most often when descending.

The Shore Lark is a very pretty and uncommon winter visitor, nearly always found only on the east coast of England. It rarely wanders far from the shore, feeding in small parties among seaweed and at the tide edge. Distinctive features are the colouring and the ' horns ' on the cock's head; these are little feathers erected when the bird is anxious or excited. Unlike other larks it is not an outstanding singer, being capable of no more than a thin "tseep" or a single bell-like call note. The Shore Lark breeds in Lapland, Siberia and other parts of Arctic Europe.

Grey Lag Goose

Geese are large, heavy, web-footed birds, and powerful fliers which in flight usually adopt a V formation—known as a 'skein'. There are several kinds of so-called 'Grey Geese' to be found in Britain, and the Grey Lag Goose is typical of them. It is nearly three feet long and, although a few breed in northern Scotland, it is chiefly a winter visitor to the northern parts of Britain. It can usually be seen on mud-flats and estuaries, and also on moorland and stubble fields.

After the breeding season geese moult, losing all their flight feathers at the same time, and they thus have to pass through a 'flightless' period; before this happens they resort to isolated areas. They are always shy and wary birds, whose flocks post 'sentries' to warn, by 'honking', of any approaching danger. This 'honking' also takes place in flight—a wonderful sound from a skein of birds high in the sky.

Our visiting Grey Lag breed in Iceland and Scandinavia, but the birds that breed here make huge nests, built on the ground, of heather and sticks and lined partly with the downy breast feathers of the female. About five creamy white eggs are laid and these are incubated only by the female. The goslings, which can fly when about eight weeks old, are tended by both parents.

White-fronted Goose *(above)*
Pink-footed Goose *(below)*

Although the Grey Geese are all rather alike, there are certain points to look for in order to tell them apart. The Grey Lag is usually the largest, the head and neck being the same colour as the body, the bill orange, the legs flesh-coloured and the breast having a few dark spots. The White-fronted Goose is darker in general colour, barred with black below, and has a pink bill and orange feet. There is also a white area at the base of the bill which extends over the front of the face. The Pink-footed Goose has a dark head and neck, a small pink and black bill, and pink legs. General habits of these Grey Geese are the same, and all are winter visitors.

The White-fronted Goose breeds in Siberia and the Arctic areas of North America, migrating as far as the Mediterranean in winter. Its cry is somewhat higher pitched than that of other Grey Geese, louder, with a sort of laughing sound. It is said to be a little tamer.

The Pink-footed Goose nests in Iceland, Greenland and Spitzbergen. In the winter it is found chiefly on our east coast, although, like many geese, it also occurs on the River Severn.

Recognition of all Grey Geese is difficult owing to the variations in size and plumage, not only in young birds but also in adults.

Canada Goose *(below)*

Brent Goose *(above)*

There are in Britain three sorts of geese which have quite a lot of black in their plumage. The smaller two are the Brent Goose and the Barnacle Goose, which are known as Black Geese. The other is the large Canada Goose, a bird which was introduced into Europe from America more than two hundred years ago. The Canada Goose is now a resident, breeding here in suitable areas. It likes inland ponds and lakes, but can be found on marshes also. It is the largest goose breeding in Europe, and in this country is now most plentiful in east and south-east England. It nests, often on a small island, in a hollow on the ground, lined with grasses, reeds and feathers. Usually there are five or six eggs, but large clutches of ten or more have been known. Incubation is by the goose—with the gander acting as sentry.

The Brent Goose is a winter visitor, becoming scarcer; it is chiefly found on the east coast. There are two forms, one with a dark breast and the other pale. They breed in the Arctic. The call of Brent Geese is a hoarse 'kronk'.

The Barnacle Goose (not illustrated) is found as a winter visitor to the west coast of Scotland and in Ireland.

Shelduck ***(duck and drake, above)***

Eider ***(duck and drake, below)***

Several kinds of ducks prefer the sea and the coast to inland waters, and are known as marine ducks.

The Shelduck likes sandy coasts and spends some time at sea, although never very far out. It feeds on shrimps, shellfish and worms, picked up at the edge of the tide. This duck is a resident, occurring on most suitable coasts, but before the moulting season most of the adults converge on the area of the Bristol Channel or cross the North Sea to Heligoland.

Shelduck often come inland to breed, selecting an old rabbit burrow as a nesting site. The nest itself is made almost completely of down feathers, and a very big clutch of eggs—sometimes up to twenty—is laid. The usual number is about ten, and there is only one brood.

A more marine species of duck is the Eider—a bird with striking plumage and a curiously shaped bill. Found chiefly on Scottish coasts, it is now increasing in numbers in England and Wales. The Eider, rather a tame bird, flies low over the water, and feeds more by diving for small fish, shrimps and small crabs than by picking up shellfish etc. from the sand. It nests in colonies, generally concealed by vegetation or rocks; and about five eggs are laid in a nest made of grass and seaweed, lined with feathers.

The male makes a curious cooing sound when courting.

Red-breasted Merganser *(below)*

Sand Martin *(above)*

Another marine duck is the Red-breasted Merganser, a member of a group known as 'Saw-bill Ducks' because of the toothed edges to the bill. This bill is specially adapted for catching and holding fish, which are caught by diving, by swimming under water or by swimming on the surface with the head and neck submerged.

This bird is resident in Scotland and parts of northern England, but elsewhere is a winter visitor. It breeds near rivers or lakes, sometimes in woods, but always on the ground under some kind of shelter. The number of eggs varies between seven and fifteen, and there is one brood. Rather silent birds, Mergansers are best identified by the long, thin bill, and by the crest at the back of the head.

The Sand Martin is the smallest member of the British swallow family, and visits this country in summer. It is found inland, near river banks and gravel pits, just as much as on the sandy coast. Like other martins it spends much time in the air, catching insects in flight. It nests in colonies, making for itself a burrow about two feet long, at the end of which four or five white eggs are laid. There are two broods.

In the autumn, like the other members of its family, it leaves us for southern Europe and North Africa.

INDEX